Italian Dialogues for Beginners
Book 4

Over 100 Daily Used Phrases and Short Stories to Learn Italian in Your Car. Have Fun and Grow Your Vocabulary with Crazy Effective Language Learning Lessons

www.LearnLikeNatives.com

www.LearnLikeNatives.com

© Copyright 2020
By Learn Like A Native

ALL RIGHTS RESERVED

No part of this book may be reproduced, stored in a retrieval system, or transmitted in any form or by any means, without the prior written permission of the publisher.

www.LearnLikeNatives.com

TABLE OF CONTENT

INTRODUCTION	5
CHAPTER 1 The Driver's License / question words	17
Translation of the Story	35
The Driver's License	35
CHAPTER 2 At the Travel Agency / likes and dislikes	47
Translation of the Story	66
At the Travel Agency	66
CHAPTER 3 Valentine's Day in Paris / prepositions	79
Translation of the Story	98
Valentine's Day in Paris	98
CONCLUSION	109
About the Author	115

www.LearnLikeNatives.com

www.LearnLikeNatives.com

INTRODUCTION

Before we dive into some Italian, I want to congratulate you, whether you're just beginning, continuing, or resuming your language learning journey. Here at Learn Like a Native, we understand the determination it takes to pick up a new language and after reading this book, you'll be another step closer to achieving your language goals.

As a thank you for learning with us, we are giving you free access to our 'Speak Like a Native' eBook. It's packed full of practical advice and insider tips on how to make language learning quick, easy, and most importantly, enjoyable. Head over to LearnLikeNatives.com to access your free guide and peruse our huge selection of language learning resources.

Learning a new language is a bit like cooking—you need several different ingredients and the right technique, but the end result is sure to be delicious. We created this book of short stories for learning Italian because language is alive. Language is about the senses—hearing, tasting the words on your tongue, and touching another culture up close. Learning a language in a classroom is a fine place to start, but it's not a complete introduction to a language.

In this book, you'll find a language come to life. These short stories are miniature immersions into the Italian language, at a level that is perfect for beginners. This book is not a lecture on grammar. It's not an endless vocabulary list. This book is the closest you can come to a language immersion without leaving the country. In the stories within, you will see people speaking to each other, going through daily life situations, and using the most common, helpful words and phrases in language.

You are holding the key to bringing your Italian studies to life.

Made for Beginners

We made this book with beginners in mind. You'll find that the language is simple, but not boring. Most of the book is in the present tense, so you will be able to focus on dialogues, root verbs, and understand and find patterns in subject-verb agreement.

This is not "just" a translated book. While reading novels and short stories translated into Italian is a wonderful thing, beginners (and even novices) often run into difficulty. Literary licenses and complex sentence structure can make reading in your second language truly difficult—not to mention BORING. That's why Italian Short

Stories for Beginners is the perfect book to pick up. The stories are simple, but not infantile. They were not written for children, but the language is simple so that beginners can pick it up.

The Benefits of Learning a Second Language

If you have picked up this book, it's likely that you are already aware of the many benefits of learning a second language. Besides just being fun, knowing more than one language opens up a whole new world to you. You will be able to communicate with a much larger chunk of the world. Opportunities in the workforce will open up, and maybe even your day-to-day work will be improved.

www.LearnLikeNatives.com

Improved communication can also help you expand your business. And from a neurological perspective, learning a second language is like taking your daily vitamins and eating well, for your brain!

How To Use The Book

The chapters of this book all follow the same structure:

- A short story with several dialogs
- A summary in Italian
- A list of important words and phrases and their English translation
- Questions to test your understanding
- Answers to check if you were right
- The English translation of the story to clear every doubt

You may use this book however is comfortable for you, but we have a few recommendations for getting the most out of the experience. Try these tips and if they work for you, you can use them on every chapter throughout the book.

1) Start by reading the story all the way through. Don't stop or get hung up on any particular words or phrases. See how much of the plot you can understand in this way. We think you'll get a lot more of it than you may expect, but it is completely normal not to understand everything in the story. You are learning a new language, and that takes time.

2) Read the summary in Italian. See if it matches what you have understood of the plot.

3) Read the story through again, slower this time. See if you can pick up the meaning of any words or phrases you don't understand

by using context clues and the information from the summary.

4) Test yourself! Try to answer the five comprehension questions that come at the end of each story. Write your answers down, and then check them against the answer key. How did you do? If you didn't get them all, no worries!

5) Look over the vocabulary list that accompanies the chapter. Are any of these the words you did not understand? Did you already know the meaning of some of them from your reading?

6) Now go through the story once more. Pay attention this time to the words and phrases you haven't understand. If you'd like, take the time to look them up to expand your meaning of the story. Every time you read over the story, you'll understand more and more.

7) Move on to the next chapter when you are ready.

Read and Listen

The audio version is the best way to experience this book, as you will hear a native Italian speaker tell you each story. You will become accustomed to their accent as you listen along, a huge plus for when you want to apply your new language skills in the real world.

If this has ignited your language learning passion and you are keen to find out what other resources are available, go to LearnLikeNatives.com, where you can access our vast range of free learning materials. Don't know where to begin? An excellent place to start is our 'Speak Like a Native' free eBook, full of practical advice and insider tips on how to make language learning quick, easy, and most importantly, enjoyable.

And remember, small steps add up to great advancements! No moment is better to begin learning than the present.

www.LearnLikeNatives.com

FREE BOOK!

Get the *FREE BOOK* that reveals the secrets path to learn any language fast, and without leaving your country.

Discover:

- The **language 5 golden rules** to master languages at will

- Proven **mind training techniques** to revolutionize your learning

- A complete step-by-step guide to **conquering any language**

www.LearnLikeNatives.com

www.LearnLikeNatives.com

CHAPTER 1
The Driver's License / question words

STORIA

Wayne vive in una Metropoli. Wayne ha quarant'anni. Di solito va a lavorare in auto. Wayne oggi è in ritardo per andare al lavoro. Wayne va sempre più veloce. Guida oltre il limite di velocità. Ha bisogno di arrivare al lavoro in tempo. Oggi ha una riunione importante.

Wayne sente un suono. Guarda dietro di lui. C'è una macchina della polizia dietro di lui. Oh, no, pensa. Sto andando piuttosto veloce. Accosta la macchina. Anche la macchina della polizia si ferma. Un poliziotto scende. Va verso la macchina di Wayne.

"Salve", dice l'agente di polizia.

"Salve, signore", dice Wayne.

"**Perché** pensi che ti abbia fermato?" chiede il poliziotto.

"Non lo so. Quale legge sto infrangendo?" chiede Wayne.

"Stai andando troppo veloce", dice il poliziotto.

"**Quanti** chilometri all'ora sono oltre il limite di velocità?" chiede Wayne.

"Basta", dice il poliziotto. "**Dove** vai così di fretta?"

"Al lavoro", dice Wayne.

"Mostrami la tua patente", dice l'ufficiale. Wayne tira fuori il portafoglio. Lo apre. Tira fuori la sua patente. La dà all'agente di polizia.

"Questa è scaduta", dice l'ufficiale. "Sei in grossi guai." L'ufficiale dice a Wayne che non può guidare con una patente scaduta. Wayne deve fare una nuova patente. Wayne accetta. L'ufficiale gli dice che non può guidare per andare al lavoro oggi. Wayne deve arrangiarsi senza la macchina.

Wayne non può più guidare la sua auto. Ora va a lavorare in altri modi. Può scegliere tra il treno o l'autobus. A volte, guida la sua bicicletta. Se è in ritardo, prende un taxi. Oggi è di nuovo in ritardo.

Wayne arriva in ufficio.

"Ciao, Wayne," dice il suo collega, Xavier. "**Come** sei arrivato qui? La tua patente è scaduta, giusto?"

"Sì, lo è," dice Wayne. "Oggi sono in taxi. **Quanto dista** la tua casa da qui?" Xavier di solito va al lavoro a piedi.

"La mia casa è a un chilometro di distanza", dice Xavier. "**Quanto ci metti** ad arrivare col taxi?"

"Circa venti minuti", dice Wayne.

"Non male", dice Xavier. "E **quanto costa** il taxi?"

"Circa venti dollari", dice Wayne.

"Oh, questo è un po' costoso", dice Xavier. "Quale compagnia di taxi è?

"Birmingham Taxi", dice Wayne. "Perché sei così interessato?"

"La mia famiglia possiede una compagnia di taxi," dice Xavier. "Mio fratello la gestisce."

"Bello", dice Wayne. "Posso avere un passaggio gratis?" Entrambi ridono. Wayne sta scherzando. Ma ha bisogno di risolvere il suo problema. Non può pagare un taxi ogni giorno. L'indomani, decide di rifare la patente.

Il giorno dopo, Wayne prende l'autobus per la motorizzazione, il Dipartimento dei Veicoli a Motore. Questo è l'edificio dove la gente ottiene la patente di guida. Esce dalla sua auto. C'è una linea fuori. Molte persone devono fare la patente. L'ufficio è lento. Si mette in fila. Dopo un'ora, è dentro l'edificio. C'è un'altra fila. Aspetta.

"**Chi** è il prossimo?" chiede la donna.

"Io", dice Wayne.

"Bene, venga!" dice. È impaziente. "Di **cosa** hai bisogno?"

"Ho bisogno di rinnovare la mia patente", dice Wayne.

"Mi dia la sua vecchia patente", dice.

"Non ce l'ho", dice Wayne. Lo fissa. Sembra arrabbiata.

"**Perché non** ce l'ha con sé?" chiede.

"Non riesco a trovarla", dice Wayne.

"**Con chi** sto parlando?" chiede.

"Cosa vuole dire?" chiede Wayne. È confuso.

"Ok, ragazzo intelligente, dimmi il tuo nome e cognome", dice.

"Quanti anni hai?" chiede.

"Perché?" chiede Wayne.

"Devo confermare la tua data di nascita", dice. **"Quando** sei nato?"

Wayne glielo dice. Guarda il suo computer. Ci mette molto tempo. Scuote la testa.

"Non riesco a trovarti," dice. "C'è un problema con il sistema oggi. Torna domani."

"Non posso", dice Wayne.

"Se vuoi la patente oggi, dovrai superare l'esame di guida", dice.

"**Come mai?**" chiede Wayne.

"Il computer dice che non hai la patente," esclama. Wayne ha bisogno della sua patente oggi. Va all'altra fila. Farà il suo esame di guida. Facile, pensa. Sa come guidare. Tutte le altre persone sono adolescenti. Lui è il più vecchio in questa fila.

"**A chi tocca**?" chiede un grand'uomo con un completo marrone.

"A me," dice Wayne. Segue il grande uomo sulla sua auto. Entrano in macchina. Wayne cerca di ricordare tutto quello che fai in un esame di guida. Controlla gli specchietti. Si mette la cintura di sicurezza. Vede l'esaminatore che scrive su un blocco note.

"Ok, andiamo", dice l'esaminatore.

Wayne esce con attenzione dal parcheggio. Guida lentamente. Usa la freccia. Prende la strada e guida sotto il limite di velocità. L'esaminatore lo dirige attraverso la città. Wayne si assicura di fermarsi quando il semaforo è giallo, e di utilizzare la freccia. Wayne fa un buon lavoro.

Wayne pensa di aver superato l'esame. L'esaminatore lo dirige di nuovo alla motorizzazione. Tuttavia, l'esaminatore gli dice di fermarsi.

"Ora devi parcheggiare in parallelo", dice l'esaminatore. Wayne non parcheggia mai in parallelo. È nervoso. L'esaminatore lo indirizza verso un piccolo parcheggio. Wayne parcheggia l'auto nello spazio. Ha quasi finito di parcheggiare. Ma poi sente un suono "ding". La sua auto colpisce l'auto dietro di lui.

"Oh, no", dice Wayne.

"Questo errore invalida automaticamente l'esame," dice l'esaminatore. "Mi dispiace, hai fallito l'esame per la patente."

Wayne esce dall'auto per lasciare che l'esaminatore riporti l'auto in ufficio.

"**Quanti** anni hai guidato?" chiede l'esaminatore.

"Ventiquattro", dice Wayne. Si vergogna. Deve tornare domani.

RIASSUNTO

Wayne ha una patente di guida. È scaduta. Wayne deve prendere taxi, autobus e altre forme di trasporto per andare al lavoro. Decide di rinnovare la sua patente. Va alla motorizzazione per farlo. Aspetta in una lunga fila e deve rispondere a un sacco di domande. C'è un problema con il sistema informatico. Wayne deve rifare l'esame di guida da zero. Fa un buon lavoro con l'esaminatore in macchina. Tuttavia, Wayne non supera il suo test perché ha urtato una macchina durante il parcheggio in parallelo.

LISTA DI VOCABOLI

Perchè	why
Quale	which
Quanti	how many
Dove	where
Come	how
Quanto dista	how far
Quanto ci metti	how long does it take

Quanto costa	how much does it cost
Chi	who
Cosa	what
Perchè non	why don't
Con chi	with whom
Quanti anni	how old
Quando	when
Come mai	how come
Di chi	whose

www.LearnLikeNatives.com

DOMANDE

1) Perché Wayne viene fermato dal poliziotto?

    a) accende una luce rossa

    b) la sua auto è rotta

    c) sta andando troppo veloce

    d) è un criminale

2) Wayne si mette in grossi guai con l'ufficiale perché...

    a) la sua patente è scaduta

    b) la sua auto non è registrata

    c) sputa sul poliziotto

    d) non risponde al poliziotto

3) Quale di questi mezzi di trasporto costa $20 affinché Wayne arrivi al lavoro?

   a) bicicletta

   b) autobus

   c) treno

   d) taxi

4) Wayne non appare nel sistema informatico alla motorizzazione. Perché?

   a) non ha mai avuto una patente

   b) ha una brutta giornata

   c) c'è un problema con il sistema informatico

   d) la sua data di nascita è sbagliata

5) Perché Wayne non supera il test?

a) è la prima volta alla guida

b) parcheggia male perché va a sbattere contro un'altra macchina

c) parcheggia male perché l'auto è troppo grande

d) è ubriaco

RISPOSTE

1) Perché Wayne viene fermato dal poliziotto?

c) sta andando troppo veloce

2) Wayne si mette in grossi guai con l'ufficiale perché...

a) la sua patente è scaduta

3) Quale di questi mezzi di trasporto costa $20 affinché Wayne arrivi al lavoro?

    d) taxi

4) Wayne non appare nel sistema informatico alla motorizzazione. Perché?

    c) c'è un problema con il sistema informatico

5) Perché Wayne non supera il test?

    b) parcheggia male perché va a sbattere contro un'altra macchina

Translation of the Story

The Driver's License

STORY

Wayne lives in a city. Wayne is forty years old. He usually drives his car to work. Wayne is late to work today. Wayne drives faster and faster. He drives over the speed limit. He needs to get to work on time. Today he has an important meeting.

Wayne hears a sound. He looks behind him. There is a police car behind him. Oh, no, he thinks. I am going rather fast. He stops the car. The police car stops, too. A policeman gets out. He walks over to Wayne's car.

"Hello," says the police officer.

"Hello, sir," says Wayne.

"**Why** do you think I pulled you over?" asks the policeman.

"I don't know. **Which** law am I breaking?" asks Wayne.

"You are going way too fast," says the policeman.

"**How many** kilometers per hour am I over the speed limit?" asks Wayne.

"Enough," says the policeman. "**Where** are you going in such a hurry?"

"To work," says Wayne.

"Show me your driver's license," says the officer. Wayne takes out his wallet. He opens it. He pulls out his driver's license. He gives it to the police officer.

"This is expired," says the officer. "You're in big trouble." The officer tells Wayne he can't drive with an expired license. Wayne must get a new license. Wayne agrees. The officer tells him he can't drive to work today. Wayne must live without a car.

Wayne has to stop driving his car. Now he goes to work other ways. He can choose between the train or the bus. Sometimes, he rides his bike. If he is late, he takes a taxi. Today, he is late again.

Wayne arrives to the office.

"Hi, Wayne," says his colleague, Xavier. "**How** did you get here? Your license is expired, right?"

"Yes, it is," says Wayne. "Today I am in taxi. **How far** is your house from here?" Xavier usually walks to work.

"My house is a kilometer away," says Xavier. "**How long** does a taxi take to get here?"

"Oh, about twenty minutes," says Wayne.

"Not bad," says Xavier. "And **how much** does the taxi cost?"

"About twenty dollars," says Wayne.

"Oh, that is a bit expensive," says Xavier. "Which taxi company is it?

"Birmingham Taxi," says Wayne. "Why are you so interested?"

"My family owns a taxi company," says Xavier. "My brother runs it."

"Nice," says Wayne. "Can I get a free ride?" They both laugh. Wayne is kidding. But he needs to solve his problem. He can't pay for a taxi every day. He decides tomorrow he is going to get his license.

The next day, Wayne takes the bus to the DMV, the Department of Motor Vehicles. This is the building where people get their driver's license. He gets out of his car. There is a line outside. Many people have to get their license. The office is slow. He gets in the line. After an hour, he is inside the building. There is another line. He waits.

"**Who** is next?" asks the woman.

"Me," says Wayne.

"Well, come on!" she says. She is impatient. "**What** do you need?"

"I need to renew my license," says Wayne.

"Give me your old card," she says.

"I don't have it," says Wayne. She stares at him. She seems angry.

"**Why don't** you have it?" she asks.

"I can't find it," says Wayne.

"**With whom** am I speaking?" she asks.

"What do you mean?" asks Wayne. He is confused.

"Ok, smart guy, tell me your first and last name," she says. Wayne tells her.

"**How old** are you?" she asks.

"**What for**?" asks Wayne.

"I have to confirm your birth date," she says. "**When** were you born?"

Wayne tells her. She looks at her computer. She takes a long time. She shakes her head.

"I can't find you," she says. "There is a problem with the system today. Come back tomorrow."

"I can't," says Wayne.

"If you want your license today, you will have to take the driving test over," she says.

"**How come**?" asks Wayne.

"The computer says you have no license," she says. Wayne needs his license today. He goes to the other line. He will take his driver's test. Easy, he thinks. He knows how to drive. All the other people are teenagers. He is the oldest in this line.

"**Whose** turn is it?" asks a big man with a brown suit.

"Mine," says Wayne. He follows the big man to his car. They get in the car. Wayne tries to remember everything you do in a driver's test. He checks the mirrors. He puts on his seatbelt. He sees the examiner writing on a notepad.

"Okay, let's go," says the examiner.

Wayne carefully backs out of the parking space. He drives slowly. He uses his turn signal. He gets on the road and drives under the speed limit. The examiner directs him through the town. Wayne makes sure to stop at yellow lights and to use his blinker. Wayne does a good job.

Wayne thinks he passes. The examiner directs him back to the DMV. However, the examiner tells him to stop.

"Now you must parallel park," says the examiner. Wayne never parallel parks. He is nervous. The examiner directs him to a tiny parking space. Wayne turns the car into the space. He is almost finished parking. But then he hears a 'ding' sound. His car hits the car behind him.

"Oh, no," says Wayne.

"That is an automatic fail," says the examiner. "Sorry, you fail your driver's test."

Wayne gets out of the car to let the examiner drive the car back to the office.

"**How many** years have you been driving?" asks the examiner.

"Twenty-four," says Wayne. He is ashamed. He has to come back tomorrow.

CHAPTER 2
At the Travel Agency / likes and dislikes

STORIA

Yolanda e Zelda sono sorelle. E sono molto impegnate nella vita. Entrambe vivono a New York City. Yolanda è una parrucchiera per persone famose. Zelda è un avvocato e ha due figli. Sono così occupate che a volte non si vedono per mesi.

Yolanda un giorno ha un'idea e Chiama Zelda.

"Zelda, cara! Come stai?" chiede.

"Bene, sorella", dice Zelda. "Come stai?"

"Benone! Ho avuto un'idea meravigliosa," dice Yolanda. "**Dovremmo** fare un viaggio insieme!"

"Che bella idea," dice Zelda. "**Mi piace**! Dove?"

"Non lo so, d'ovunque parte," dice Yolanda. "Non importa dove! **Mi piacerebbe** andare ovunque con te!"

"Andiamo all'agenzia viaggi domani," dice Zelda. "Possono aiutarci."

Le due sorelle si incontrano il giorno dopo. Zelda porta diverse pagine di ricerca sulle vacanze. Le pagine parlano di diversi tipi di turismo. C'è il turismo ricreativo, come rilassarsi e divertirsi in spiaggia. C'è il turismo culturale, come visite turistiche o visitare musei per conoscere la storia e l'arte. Il turismo di avventura invece, è per la gente che **adora** esplorare i posti distanti e le attività estreme. L'ecoturismo in ultimo consiste nel viaggiare in ambienti naturali.

Yolanda legge le pagine di ricerca. Il turismo della salute è viaggiare per prendersi cura del corpo e della mente visitando luoghi come località termali. Il turismo religioso è un viaggio per celebrare eventi religiosi o visitare importanti luoghi di culto.

"Ci sono così tanti tipi di viaggio", dice Yolanda.

"Sì", dice Zelda. "**Mi piace** viaggiare per un motivo. Non riesco a stare sdraiata sulla spiaggia a non fare nulla." Yolanda ama la spiaggia. Le piace non fare niente in vacanza. Ma non dice niente.

Le sorelle arrivano all'agenzia di viaggi. L'agente di viaggi è una donna. Sembra simpatica. Yolanda e Zelda si siedono con lei.

"Come posso aiutarvi?" chiede l'agente.

"Vorremmo fare un viaggio", dice Yolanda.

"Che tipo di viaggio?" chiede l'agente.

"**Vado pazza per la cultura**", dice Zelda. "Amo i musei. Amo l'arte."

"**Preferirei** andare da qualche parte con il sole. Amo le attività all'aria aperta", dice Yolanda.

"La gente viaggia per molte ragioni", dice l'agente. "Che ne dite di Barcellona?"

"Oh, non lo so", dice Zelda. "**Non sopporto** di non conoscere la lingua locale."

"Non parliamo spagnolo", dice Yolanda.

"Vi piacerebbe Parigi?" chiede l'agente. "Ci sono ottimi musei e ristoranti."

"Non parliamo nemmeno francese!" dicono entrambe.

"Che ne dite di Londra?" chiede l'agente.

"Fantastico!" dice Zelda.

"Così piovoso!" dice Yolanda allo stesso tempo. Le sorelle si guardano.

"Hai detto che non ti importava Yoli!" dice Zelda.

"Voglio viaggiare con te", dice Yolanda. "**Non sono arrabbiata** per Londra. Però **detesto** la pioggia!"

"Andiamo, Yolanda," dice Zelda. "Per favore!"

L'agente mostra le foto delle donne di Londra. Vedono i famosi edifici. Yolanda vorrebbe vedere il Big Ben. Zelda è entusiasta del museo d'arte Tate Modern.

"Che tipo di hotel vi piacerebbe?" chiede l'agente.

"Potremmo prendere un appartamento Airbnb", dice Yolanda.

"No, detesto stare nelle case degli altri", dice Zelda.

"Abbiamo bellissimi hotel nel centro della città", dice l'agente.

"Sembra fantastico", dice Zelda.

Zelda preferisce gli hotel di lusso. Sa che Yolanda **non ama molto** gli hotel di lusso. Ma Zelda non va mai in vacanza. Vuole che questa vacanza sia perfetta. L'agenzia di viaggi mostra le foto delle sorelle. Le camere dell'hotel sono enormi. Alcuni hanno un bagno in mezzo alla stanza.

"Sono bellissime", dice Zelda. "Ti dispiace se restiamo in un hotel di lusso, Yolanda?"

"**Niente affatto**," dice Yolanda. Zelda sa che **non le piacciono** gli hotel di lusso. Yolanda si sente triste. Zelda fa quello che vuole.

"**Cosa vi piacerebbe** fare mentre sei a Londra?" chiede l'agente di viaggio.

"Ci piacerebbe andare in tutti i musei, visitare il Palazzo e visitare alcune gallerie d'arte", dice Zelda.

"Ok", dice l'agente di viaggio. "Probabilmente è abbastanza per passare il tempo a Londra."

Yolanda non dice niente. Le sorelle pagano e lasciano l'agente di viaggio. Zelda è felice. Yolanda vorrebbe che la vacanza fosse più nel suo stile. Torna a casa. Pensa al viaggio. Sorride. Ha un piano.

Il giorno dopo, Yolanda torna all'agenzia di viaggi.

"Oh salve, Yolanda," dice l'agente. "Come posso aiutarti?"

"**Vogliamo** cambiare un po' il nostro viaggio", dice Yolanda.

"Nessun problema", dice l'agente di viaggio.

"**Preferiremmo** andare in un posto soleggiato", dice Yolanda.

"Naturalmente", dice l'agente di viaggio. L'agente di viaggio suggerisce molte posizioni diverse. Yolanda firma alcuni nuovi documenti. E dà i soldi all'agente per il cambiamento. Immagina Zelda in vacanza. sorride. Zelda ama le sorprese.

È il fine settimana. È l'ora del viaggio di Yolanda e Zelda. Le sorelle si incontrano all'aeroporto. Sono emozionate. Yolanda è nervosa.

"Ti ho portato il caffè", dice. Zelda prende il caffè.

"Grazie", dice. Prende un sorso. "Oh, ma **odio** lo zucchero nel caffè, Yoli!"

Yolanda si scusa. Prende entrambi i caffè in mano. Ora non può più portare la sua valigia.

Le due sorelle passano attraverso i controlli di sicurezza. Aspettano di salire a bordo dell'aereo. Lo schermo dice "Volo 361 per Londra / Con collegamenti / British Airways". Yolanda sorride mentre salgono sull'aereo.

Il volo dura sei ore. Yolanda e Zelda dormono. Si svegliano mentre l'aereo arriva all'aeroporto di Londra. L'assistente di volo utilizza l'altoparlante. "Se soggiornate a Londra o avete un collegamento, siete pregati di alzarvi e lasciare l'aereo."

Zelda si alza. Yolanda no.

"Andiamo, Yolanda", dice Zelda. Yolanda non si muove.

"Andiamo!" dice Zelda.

"In realtà, sorellina," dice Yolanda. "C'è un cambiamento di programma. Restiamo su questo aereo."

Zelda sembra un po' confusa.

L'assistente di volo utilizza di nuovo l'altoparlante. "Se si viaggia fino alla nostra prossima destinazione, rimanere ai vostri posti. Prossima fermata-Fiji!"

RIASSUNTO

Due sorelle, Yolanda e Zelda, vogliono fare un viaggio insieme. Vanno all'agenzia di viaggi. Sono molto diverse. E 'difficile per loro concordare su un luogo. Zelda ama pianificare le vacanze e vedere l'arte e la cultura. Yolanda preferisce spiagge e mare. Infine, decidono dove andare. Ma il giorno dopo, Yolanda torna all'agenzia di viaggi e cambia la destinazione. Zelda lo scopre quando il loro aereo atterra.

LISTA DI VOCABOLI

Dovremmo	we should
Mi piace / amo	I love
Mi piacerebbe	I would love
Adoro	I adore
Detesto	I can't stand
Ci piacerebbe	we would like
Vado pazzo per	I'm crazy about
Preferisco	I prefer
Non sopporto	I can't bear
Ti piacerebbe	would you like

www.LearnLikeNatives.com

Non sono arrabbiato per	I'm not mad about
Odio	I loathe
Non le piace	doesn't like
Molto	very much
Niente affatto	not at all
Non ama	dislikes
Cosa ti piacerebbe	what would you like
Vogliamo /vorremmo	we want
Preferiremmo	we would rather
Piace	likes

DOMANDE

1) Come si conoscono Yolanda e Zelda?

    a) sono amiche

    b) sono sorelle

    c) lavorano insieme

    d) sono vicine di casa

2) Cosa fa Zelda in vacanza?

    a) va a vedere arte e cultura

    b) si sdraia sulla spiaggia

    c) si rilassa

    d) vede cosa succede senza pianificare

3) Quale delle seguenti cose decide Yolanda al primo incontro all'agenzia viaggi?

   a) dove andare

   b) dove dormire

   c) cosa fare

   d) nessuna di queste

4) Cosa fa Yolanda quando va all'agenzia di viaggi per la seconda volta?

   a) chiede la restituzione del denaro

   b) annulla il viaggio

   c) modifica la destinazione

   d) chiama Zelda

5) Cosa succede quando le sorelle atterrano a Londra?

a) vanno al loro hotel

b) vanno in un museo

c) l'aereo si schianta

d) Yolanda sorprende Zelda con una nuova destinazione

RISPOSTE

1) Come si conoscono Yolanda e Zelda?

b) sono sorelle

2) Cosa fa Zelda in vacanza?

a) va a vedere arte e cultura

3) Quale delle seguenti decisioni decide Yolanda al primo incontro con l'agenzia di viaggi?

    d) nessuna di queste

4) Cosa fa Yolanda quando va all'agenzia di viaggi per la seconda volta?

    c) modifica la destinazione

5) Cosa succede quando le sorelle atterrano a Londra?

    d) Yolanda sorprende Zelda con una nuova destinazione

Translation of the Story

At the Travel Agency

STORY

Yolanda and Zelda are sisters. They have very busy lives. They both live in New York City. Yolanda is a hairdresser for celebrities. Zelda is a lawyer and has two children. They are so busy, sometimes they don't see each other for months.

Yolanda has an idea one day. She calls Zelda.

"Zelda, dear! How are you?" she asks.

"Fine, sis," says Zelda. "How are you?"

"Great! I've had a marvelous idea," says Yolanda. "**We should** take a trip together!"

"What a great idea," says Zelda. "**I love** it! Where to?"

"I don't know, anywhere," says Yolanda. "Wherever! **I would love** to go anywhere with you!"

"Let's go to the travel agency tomorrow," says Zelda. "They can help."

The sisters meet the next day. Zelda brings pages of research on vacations. The pages talk about different types of tourism. There is recreational tourism, like relaxing and having fun at the beach. There's cultural tourism like sightseeing or visiting museums to learn about history and art.

Adventure tourism is for people who **adore** exploring distant places and extreme activities. Ecotourism is traveling to natural environments.

Yolanda reads the papers. Health tourism is travel to look after your body and mind by visiting places like spa resorts. Religious tourism is travel to celebrate religious events or visit important religious places.

"There are so many types of travel," says Yolanda.

"Yes," says Zelda. "**I enjoy** traveling for a reason. I can't stand lying on the beach, doing nothing." Yolanda likes the beach. She likes doing nothing on vacation. She doesn't say anything.

The sisters arrive to the travel agency. The travel agent is a woman. She seems nice. Yolanda and Zelda sit down with her.

"How can I help you?" asks the agent.

"We would like to take a trip," says Yolanda.

"What kind of trip?" asks the agent.

"**I'm crazy about** culture," says Zelda. "I love museums. I love art."

"**I would rather** go somewhere with sunshine. I love outdoor activities," says Yolanda.

"People travel for lots of reasons," says the agent. "How about Barcelona?"

"Oh, I don't know," says Zelda. "**I can't bear** not knowing the local language."

"We don't speak Spanish," says Yolanda.

"Would you like Paris?" asks the agent. "There are very good museums and restaurants."

"We don't speak French, either!" they both say.

"How about London?" asks the agent.

"Great!" says Zelda.

"So rainy!" says Yolanda at the same time. The sisters look at each other.

"You said you don't care Yoli!" says Zelda.

"I want to travel with you," says Yolanda. "**I'm not mad about** London, though. **I detest** the rain!"

"Come on, Yolanda," says Zelda. "Please!"

The agent shows the women pictures of London. They see the famous buildings. Yolanda would like to see Big Ben. Zelda is excited about the Tate Modern art museum.

"What kind of hotel would you like?" asks the agent.

"We could get an Airbnb apartment," says Yolanda.

"No, **I loathe** staying in other people's homes," says Zelda.

"We have beautiful hotels in the center of the city," says the agent.

"That sounds great," says Zelda.

Zelda prefers luxurious hotels. She knows Yolanda **doesn't like** fancy hotels **very much**. But Zelda never goes on vacation. She wants this vacation to be perfect. The travel agent shows the sisters pictures. The hotel rooms are huge. Some have a bath in the middle of the room.

"Those are gorgeous," says Zelda. "Do you mind if we stay in a fancy hotel, Yolanda?"

"**Not at all**," says Yolanda. Zelda knows she **dislikes** fancy hotels. Yolanda feels sad. Zelda does what she wants.

"**What would you like** to do while in London?" asks the travel agent.

"We would love to go to all the museums, visit the Palace, and visit some art galleries," says Zelda.

"Okay," says the travel agent. "That's probably enough to fill your time in London."

Yolanda doesn't say anything. The sisters pay and leave the travel agent. Zelda is happy. Yolanda wishes the vacation was more her style. She goes home. She thinks about the trip. She smiles. She has a plan.

The next day, Yolanda returns to the travel agent.

"Oh hello, Yolanda," says the agent. "How can I help you?"

"**We want** to change our trip a bit," says Yolanda.

"No problem," says the travel agent.

"**We would rather** go to somewhere sunny," says Yolanda.

"Of course," says the travel agent. The travel agent suggests many different locations. Yolanda signs some new papers. She gives the agent money for the change. She imagines Zelda on vacation. She smiles. Zelda **likes** surprises.

It is the weekend. It is time for Yolanda and Zelda's trip. The sisters meet at the airport. They are excited. Yolanda is nervous.

"I brought you coffee," she says. Zelda takes the coffee.

"Thanks," she says. She takes a sip. "Oh, but **I hate** sugar in my coffee, Yoli!"

Yolanda apologizes. She takes both coffees in her hands. Now she can't carry her suitcase.

The two sisters go through security. They wait to board the plane. The screen says "Flight 361 to London / With Connections / British Airways". Yolanda smiles as they get on the plane.

The flight lasts six hours. Yolanda and Zelda sleep. They awake as the plane pulls into the airport in London. The flight attendant uses the speaker. "If you are staying in London or have a connection, please stand and leave the plane."

Zelda stands up. Yolanda does not.

"Come on, Yolanda," says Zelda. Yolanda doesn't move.

"Let's go!" says Zelda.

"Actually, sis," says Yolanda. "There is a change of plans. We are staying on this plane."

Zelda looks confused.

The flight attendant uses the speaker again. "If you are traveling through to our next destination, remain in your seats. Next stop—Fiji!"

CHAPTER 3
Valentine's Day in Paris / prepositions

STORIA

Charles e Dana sono fidanzati. Sono innamorati. Charles vuole fare qualcosa di speciale per San Valentino. Invita Dana a Parigi. Parigi è chiamata la città dell'amore. Molte persone viaggiano a Parigi per trascorrere del tempo romantico con il loro partner. Forse sono i film, il cibo, i bellissimi edifici? Parigi è sempre romantica.

La coppia arriva a Parigi il 13 febbraio. L'aereo atterra. Sono entusiasti. Charles e Dana raccolgono i loro bagagli.

"Andiamo in albergo", dice Charles.

"Come?" chiede Dana.

"Possiamo prendere il treno per il centro città", dice Charles. **Di fronte** alla coppia c'è un'indicazione per il treno dell'aeroporto. Seguono le frecce, camminando **sotto** di esse. **Attraversano** il ponte, fino a giungere all'ingresso del treno. Vanno alla biglietteria automatica.

"Che biglietto compriamo?" chiede Dana. Entrambi fissano la macchinetta.

"Non lo so", dice Charles. "L'hotel si trova **nel** 7º arrondissement." Charles tenta di indovinare quale biglietto comprare. Lo compra e vanno al binario del treno. **Sopra** i binari, c'è un cartellone. Dice la direzione di ogni treno. Un treno si avvicina. Il cartello dice: 'centre-ville'. Salgono **sul** treno.

Quando il treno raggiunge la destinazione, **scendono** dal treno. Salgono le scale della metropolitana. Escono. La Torre Eiffel si erge **sopra** di loro.

"È bellissimo", dice Dana.

"Sì, è fantastico", dice Charles.

"Voglio arrivare **in** cima", dice Dana.

"Lo sapevi che ridipingono la torre ogni sette anni?" chiede Charles. "Con 50 tonnellate di vernice!"

"Non lo sapevo", dice Dana. Charles le dice di più sulla Torre Eiffel. Fu costruita nel 1889. Prende il nome da Gustave Eiffel, l'architetto responsabile del progetto.

Per 41 anni, è stata la struttura più alta del mondo. Ci sono molte repliche della torre **in tutto il mondo**. C'è anche una replica dalle dimensioni originali a Tokyo.

"Amo Parigi", dice Dana.

"Andiamo all'hotel", dice Charles. Camminano fino all'hotel vicino. È proprio dietro la Torre Eiffel.

Il giorno dopo è San Valentino. La coppia ha un pranzo speciale in programma. Vanno al ristorante Epicure. È uno dei ristoranti più romantici della città.

"Sei pronta?" chiede Charles.

"Sì", dice Dana. "Come ci arriviamo?" Escono **fuori** dall'hotel.

"È appena dopo gli Champs-Élysées", dice Charles. Camminano **lungo** la strada. Camminano verso il fiume. È una bella giornata.

Il sole splende. Dana nota quanto sono belli gli edifici. Sono tutti molto vecchi.

"Dovremmo avere edifici come questo in America", dice Dana.

"Sono più vecchi dell'America", dice Charles. Charles e Dana camminano **lungo** il fiume. Si tengono per mano. Parigi è una città per amanti.

Epicure è vicino al quartiere centrale dello shopping. Passano negozi come Louis Vuitton e Pierre Hermé. Dana si ferma a guardare nelle finestre. Il ristorante è **accanto** a uno dei suoi negozi preferiti.

"Per favore possiamo entrare", dice. Quando passano **attraverso** la porta di Hermes, Charles sa che è nei guai. Borse e sciarpe sono ovunque. Dana impazzisce. Prende due sciarpe da una vetrina. Afferra una shopper **tra** una collezione di borse.

"Per favore, Charles?" gli chiede. "Un piccolo souvenir di Parigi?" Charles pensa. I tre oggetti costano lo stesso del biglietto aereo per Parigi. E 'San Valentino, però. Dice di sì. Dana porta le sciarpe e la borsa alla cassa. Charles paga con la sua carta di credito. Escono dal negozio. Dana è molto contenta.

Charles e Dana continuano lungo la strada. Non vedono Epicure.

"È proprio qui", dice Charles.

"Qui dove?" chiede Dana.

"Qui," dice Charles. "È quello che dice Google Maps."

"Non lo vedo", dice Dana.

Charles chiama il ristorante sul suo cellulare. "Salve, non riusciamo a trovare il ristorante," dice. Resta in ascolto. La persona parla francese. "Parla inglese? No?" La persona riattacca.

"Non parlano inglese", dice Charles.

"Deve essere qui", dice Dana. Scorge un piccolo vicolo. Entra nel vicolo e cammina un po'.

"Eccolo", dice. Il ristorante è **all'interno** del vicolo, nascosto in fondo.

"Grazie al cielo", dice Charles. "Siamo già in ritardo!" Entrano nel ristorante.

"Avete una prenotazione?" chiede il cameriere.

"Sì", dice Charles. "Siamo un po' in ritardo. Charles."

"Seguitemi", dice il cameriere. Seguono il cameriere. Camminano tra i tavoli con tovaglie bianche. Sono i primi commensali. Il ristorante è vuoto.

"È bellissimo", dice Dana. Si siedono al loro tavolo. **Sopra** ci sono dei fiori freschi. Il loro tavolo è **accanto** al fuoco. Un lampadario dorato pende dal soffitto.

"Cosa prendete?" chiede il cameriere.

"Il pollo con i funghi, e i maccheroni con foie gras e carciofi", dice Charles.

"Consiglio i maccheroni **prima** del pollo", dice il cameriere.

"Ok", dice Charles.

"Il pollo viene servito con un contorno di insalata", dice il cameriere.

"Perfetto", dice Charles. "E per favore ci porti dello champagne." Charles ammicca al cameriere.

"Perché gli hai fatto l'occhiolino?" chiede Dana.

"Non l'ho fatto apposta!" dice Charles.

Dana e Charles sono molto felici. Il ristorante è uno dei migliori di Parigi. Ha tre stelle Michelin. Il cameriere arriva **dietro** Charles con i maccheroni. Sono molto prelibati. Hanno del tartufo nero in cima. Sono d'accordo, sono i migliori maccheroni che abbiano mai mangiato.

Il cameriere avvicina un carrello al tavolo. Ha due bicchieri, una bottiglia di champagne, e una scatola nera. Il cameriere apre il vino e lo versa per Charles e Dana. Lascia la scatola nera sul tavolo.

"Che cos'è?" chiede Dana.

"Dana, vuoi sposarmi?" chiede Charles. Solleva la parte superiore della scatola nera. **Sotto** c'è un enorme anello di diamanti. Lo mette al dito di Dana.

"Sì!" grida Dana.

Parigi è davvero la città dell'amore.

RIASSUNTO

Charles e Dana sono innamorati. Fanno un viaggio a Parigi per San Valentino. Si perdono alla ricerca del loro hotel. Non capiscono la metropolitana. Né Charles né Dana parlano francese. Charles riserva un pranzo speciale per

www.LearnLikeNatives.com

San Valentino. Dana non può resistere ai negozi di Parigi. Hanno difficoltà a trovare il ristorante. Dana trova il ristorante in un vicolo. A pranzo, Charles ha una sorpresa segreta per Dana. Che cos'è? Un segno di vero amore. Un cameriere al ristorante porta l'anello con lo champagne. Charles chiede a Dana di sposarlo.

LISTA DI VOCABOLI

Di fronte	in front of
Sotto	beneath
Attraversare/attraverso	across
In	in
Sopra	above

Dentro/nel	into
Fuori	off
In tutto il mondo	Around the world
Dietro	behind
Passato	past
Sotto	down
Verso	toward
Lungo	along
Accanto /vicino	near
Attraverso	through
Da	from

Tra/fra	amongst
Dentro	within
A	at
In mezzo	between
Su	on
Prima	before
Con	with
Dietro	behind
Sotto	below

DOMANDE

1) Chi ha avuto l'idea di andare in vacanza a Parigi?

   a) Charles

   b) il padre di Charles

   c) l'agente di viaggio

   d) Dana

2) Qual è la prima cosa che Charles e Dana vedono a Parigi?

   a) il Louvre

   b) gli Champs-Élysées

   c) l'hotel

   d) la Torre Eiffel

3) Quale altra città al mondo ha una Torre Eiffel a grandezza naturale?

a) New York

b) Tokyo

c) Dubai

d) Hong Kong

4) Dana a Sen valentino, convince Charles a fare una cosa. Che cosa?

a) a tornare a casa

b) ad andare al museo

c) a comprarle qualcosa da Hermes

d) a smettere di bere

5) Come fa Charles a dare a Dana l'anello di fidanzamento?

a) un cameriere lo porta al tavolo con lo champagne

b) lo mette nel suo gelato

c) lo prende dalla tasca

d) si inginocchia

RISPOSTE

1) Chi ha avuto l'idea di andare in vacanza a Parigi?

a) Charles

2) Qual è la prima cosa che Charles e Dana vedono a Parigi?

d) la Torre Eiffel

3) Quale altra città al mondo ha una Torre Eiffel a grandezza naturale?

    b) Tokyo

4) Dana a Sen valentino, convince Charles a fare una cosa. Che cosa?

    c) a comprarle qualcosa da Hermes

5) Come fa Charles a dare a Dana l'anello di fidanzamento?

    a) un cameriere lo porta fuori con lo champagne

Translation of the Story

Valentine's Day in Paris

STORY

Charles and Dana are boyfriend and girlfriend. They are in love. Charles wants to do something special for Valentine's Day. He invites Dana to Paris. Paris is called the city of love. Many people travel to Paris to spend romantic time with their partner. Maybe it is the movies, the food, the beautiful buildings? Paris always feels romantic.

The couple arrives to Paris on February 13. The plane lands. They are thrilled. Charles and Dana collect their baggage.

"Let's go to the hotel," says Charles.

"How?" asks Dana.

"We can take the train to the city center," says Charles. **In front of** the couple is a sign for the airport train. They follow the arrows, walking **beneath** them. They walk **across** the sky bridge, until they come to the entrance to the train. They go up to the ticket machine.

"Which ticket do we buy?" asks Dana. They both stare at the machine.

"I don't know," says Charles. "The hotel is **in** the 7th arrondissement." Charles guesses which ticket to buy. He buys it and they go to the train platform. **Above** the tracks, there is a sign. It tells where each train is going. A train approaches. The sign says 'centre-ville'. They get **into** the train.

When the train reaches the destination, they get **off** the train. They go up the metro stairs. They step outside. The Eiffel Tower stands **above** them.

"It's beautiful," says Dana.

"Yes, it's amazing," says Charles.

"I want to go **to** the top," says Dana.

"Did you know they paint the tower every seven years?" asks Charles. "With 50 tons of paint!"

"I didn't know that," says Dana. Charles tells her more about the Eiffel Tower. It was built in 1889. It is named after Gustave Eiffel, the architect in charge of the project. For 41 years, it was the tallest structure in the world. There are many replicas of the tower **around** the world. There is even a full-size replica in Tokyo.

"I love Paris," says Dana.

"Let's go to the hotel," says Charles. They walk to the nearby hotel. It is just **behind** the Eiffel Tower.

The next day is Valentine's Day. The couple has a special lunch planned. They go to the restaurant Epicure. It is one of the city's most romantic restaurants.

"Are you ready?" asks Charles.

"Yes," says Dana. "How do we get there?" They walk **out of** the hotel.

"It is just **past** the Champs-Élysées," says Charles. They walk **down** the street. They walk **toward** the river. It is a beautiful day. The sun is shining. Dana notices how beautiful the buildings are. They are all very old.

"We should have buildings like this in America," says Dana.

"They are older than America," says Charles. Charles and Dana walk **along** the river. They hold hands. Paris is a city for lovers.

Epicure is **near** the central shopping district. They pass shops like Louis Vuitton and Pierre Hermé. Dana stops to look in the windows. The restaurant is **next to** one of her favorite shops.

"Please can we go in," she says. When they go **through** the door of Hermes, Charles knows he is in trouble. Purses and scarves are everywhere. Dana goes crazy. She takes two scarves **from** a display. She grabs a bag from **amongst** a pile of purses.

"Please, Charles?" she asks him. "A little Paris souvenir?" Charles thinks. The three items cost the same as the airplane ticket to Paris. It is Valentine's Day, though. He says yes. Dana takes the scarves and the purse to the cash register. Charles pays with his credit card. They leave the shop. Dana is very content.

Charles and Dana continue down the street. They don't see Epicure.

"It is right here," says Charles.

"Right where?" asks Dana.

"Here," says Charles. "That is what Google maps says."

"I don't see it," says Dana.

Charles calls the restaurant on his cell phone. "Hello, we cannot find the restaurant," he says. He listens. The person speaks French. "Do you speak English? No?" The person hangs up.

"They don't speak English," says Charles.

"It has to be here," says Dana. She spots a small alley. She enters the alleyway and walks a bit.

"Here it is," she says. The restaurant is **within** the alleyway, hidden **at** the very end.

"Thank goodness," says Charles. "We are already late!" They enter the restaurant.

"Do you have a reservation?" asks the waiter.

"Yes," says Charles. "We are a bit late. Charles."

"Follow me," says the waiter. They follow the waiter. They walk between tables with white tablecloths. They are the first diners. The restaurant is empty.

"It's beautiful," says Dana. They sit at their table. It has fresh flowers **on** it. Their table is **beside** the fire. A golden chandelier hangs from the ceiling.

"What would you like?" asks the waiter.

"The chicken with mushrooms, and the macaroni with foie gras and artichoke," says Charles.

"I recommend the macaroni **before** the chicken," says the waiter.

"Ok," says Charles.

"The chicken is served with a side salad," says the waiter.

"Perfect," says Charles. "And please bring us some champagne." Charles winks at the waiter.

"Why did you wink at him?" asks Dana.

"I didn't mean to!" says Charles.

Dana and Charles are very happy. The restaurant is one of the best in Paris. It has three Michelin stars. The waiter comes up **behind** Charles with the macaroni. It is very rich. It has black truffle on top. They agree, it is the best macaroni they have ever had.

The waiter rolls a cart to the table. It has two glasses, a bottle of champagne, and a black box. The waiter opens the wine and pours it for Charles and Dana. He leaves the black box on the table.

"What's that?" asks Dana.

"Dana, will you marry me?" asks Charles. He lifts the top of the black box. **Below** is a huge diamond ring. He puts it on Dana's finger.

"Yes!" shouts Dana.

Paris really is the city of love.

CONCLUSION

You did it!

You finished a whole book in a brand new language. That in and of itself is quite the accomplishment, isn't it?

Congratulate yourself on time well spent and a job well done. Now that you've finished the book, you have familiarized yourself with over 500 new vocabulary words, comprehended the heart of 3 short stories, and listened to loads of dialogue unfold, all without going anywhere!

Charlemagne said "To have another language is to possess a second soul." After immersing yourself in this book, you are broadening your horizons and opening a whole new path for yourself.

Have you thought about how much you know now that you did not know before? You've learned everything from how to greet and how to express your emotions to basics like colors and place words. You can tell time and ask question. All without opening a schoolbook. Instead, you've cruised through fun, interesting stories and possibly listened to them as well.

Perhaps before you weren't able to distinguish meaning when you listened to Italian. If you used the audiobook, we bet you can now pick out meanings and words when you hear someone speaking. Regardless, we are sure you have taken an important step to being more fluent. You are well on your way!

Best of all, you have made the essential step of distinguishing in your mind the idea that most often hinders people studying a new language. By approaching Italian through our short stories and dialogs, instead of formal lessons with just grammar and vocabulary, you are no longer in the 'learning' mindset. Your approach is much more similar to an osmosis, focused on speaking and using the language, which is the end goal, after all!

So, what's next?

This is just the first of five books, all packed full of short stories and dialogs, covering essential, everyday Italian that will ensure you master the basics. You can find the rest of the books in the series, as well as a whole host of other resources, at LearnLikeNatives.com. Simply add the book to your library to take the next step in your language learning journey. If you are ever in need of new ideas or direction, refer to our 'Speak Like a Native' eBook, available to you for free at LearnLikeNatives.com, which clearly outlines practical steps you can take to continue learning any language you choose.

We also encourage you to get out into the real world and practice your Italian. You have a leg up on most beginners, after all—instead of pure textbook learning, you have been absorbing the sound and soul of the language. Do not underestimate the foundation you have built reviewing the chapters of this book. Remember, no one feels 100% confident when they speak with a native speaker in another language.

One of the coolest things about being human is connecting with others. Communicating with someone in their own language is a wonderful gift. Knowing the language turns you into a local and opens up your world. You will see the reward of learning languages for many years to come, so keep that practice up!. Don't let your fears stop you from taking the chance to use your Italian. Just give it a try, and remember that you will make mistakes. However, these mistakes will teach you so much, so view every single one as a small victory! Learning is growth.

www.LearnLikeNatives.com

Don't let the quest for learning end here! There is so much you can do to continue the learning process in an organic way, like you did with this book. Add another book from Learn Like a Native to your library. Listen to Italian talk radio. Watch some of the great Italian films. Put on the latest CD from Pavarotti. Take cooking lessons in Italian. Whatever you do, don't stop because every little step you take counts towards learning a new language, culture, and way of communicating.

www.LearnLikeNatives.com

www.LearnLikeNatives.com

www.LearnLikeNatives.com

Learn Like a Native is a revolutionary **language education brand** that is taking the linguistic world by storm. Forget boring grammar books that never get you anywhere, Learn Like a Native teaches you languages in a fast and fun way that actually works!

As an international, multichannel, language learning platform, we provide **books, audio guides and eBooks** so that you can acquire the knowledge you need, swiftly and easily.

Our **subject-based learning**, structured around real-world scenarios, builds your conversational muscle and ensures you learn the content most relevant to your requirements. Discover our tools at *LearnLikeNatives.com*.

When it comes to learning languages, we've got you covered!

www.ingramcontent.com/pod-product-compliance
Lightning Source LLC
Chambersburg PA
CBHW071742080526
44588CB00013B/2120